# Handbook of Planets and Moons

## by Josey Baker

SEEDS
OF SCIENCE

ROOTS
OF READING®

Published and Distributed by

Delta Education
...because children learn by doing.®

A member of
School Specialty
Science

Published and Distributed by

**Delta Education**
*...because children learn by doing.*®

A member of
School Specialty
*Science*

These materials are based upon work partially supported by the National Science Foundation under grant numbers ESI-0242733 and ESI-0628272. The Federal Government has certain rights in this material. Any opinions, findings, and conclusions or recommendations expressed in this material are those of the author(s) and do not necessarily reflect the views of the National Science Foundation.

Developed at Lawrence Hall of Science and the Graduate School of Education at the University of California at Berkeley

Seeds of Science/Roots of Reading® is a collaboration of a science team led by Jacqueline Barber and a literacy team led by P. David Pearson and Gina Cervetti.

Delta Education LLC
PO Box 3000
Nashua, NH 03061
1-800-258-1302
www.deltaeducation.com

Handbook of Planets and Moons
594-0058
ISBN: 978-1-59821-532-8
Printing 1 – 4/2010
Standard Printing Company, Canton, OH

# Contents

# Introduction

We live on a **planet** called Earth, which is one of the eight planets in our **Solar System**. At the center of our Solar System is the Sun, and the planets **orbit** (or **revolve** around) it. The planets orbit the Sun at different distances, and they are all different sizes. Mercury is the smallest, and Jupiter is the largest.

Many of these planets have **moons** orbiting them. For example, Saturn has at least 46 moons, and they're all different sizes. So far, more than 150 moons have been discovered in our Solar System, but scientists think there may be even more than that.

Planets and moons are also called **Solar System objects**. So far, people have visited only one Solar System object other than Earth—Earth's Moon. Still, we know a lot about what **conditions** are like on other planets and moons in our Solar System. Many other planets and moons have been explored by spacecraft without people aboard. These spacecraft have taken pictures of interesting **surface features**. **Astronomers** and other scientists learn new things about Solar System objects all the time. Sometimes, they even discover new objects.

This handbook has information on all eight planets, along with ten moons. You can find out about conditions on each one. You can also read about **missions** that have explored these objects. At the end of the book is a short section on other objects in our Solar System, such as **comets** and **asteroids**.

# Mercury

There are thousands of craters on the surface of Mercury. Some big craters have smaller craters inside them!

Mercury (MURK-yur-ee) is the smallest **planet** and the closest planet to the Sun. It **orbits** the Sun faster than any other planet. Mercury is one of the rocky planets.

## Conditions

Mercury's rocky surface is covered with **craters**—holes made by objects that hit the surface. The largest crater is about 1,300 kilometers (800 miles) across and about two kilometers (a little more than one mile) deep. There are also thousands of smaller craters.

Because Mercury is so close to the Sun, the planet gets more heat and light than planets that are farther away, such as Earth. Mercury also has no **atmosphere** to protect it from the Sun's rays. During the day, surface **temperatures** on Mercury can reach 427°C (801°F). Because there is no atmosphere to hold this heat on the surface of Mercury, at night temperatures can drop as low as -173°C (-279°F).

## Exploration

Very few **missions** have explored Mercury. The *MESSENGER* spacecraft flew past Mercury in 2008 and took more than 1,200 pictures of the planet. Now scientists have images of almost the entire surface. This mission helped scientists learn many interesting things, including what types of rocks are on Mercury's surface.

# Venus

This picture shows
lava that hardened
long ago on the
surface of Venus.

Venus (VEE-nus) comes closer to Earth in its **orbit** than any other **planet**. Other than the Sun and the Moon, Venus is the brightest object in Earth's sky. Venus is one of the rocky planets.

## Conditions

There are more than 1,000 volcanoes on the rocky surface of Venus. The biggest ones are more than 100 kilometers (about 60 miles) across! Scientists have not **observed** the volcanoes erupting yet. Other **surface features** on Venus are mountains, valleys, and **craters**—holes made by objects that hit the surface.

Clouds hide the surface of Venus. The planet's **atmosphere** is mostly **composed of** carbon dioxide gas. It is much thicker than Earth's atmosphere. Venus's atmosphere is so thick and heavy that it crushes spacecraft after just a few hours.

Venus's thick atmosphere acts like a blanket that holds in heat from the Sun. It stays very hot all the time on Venus. The **temperature** there is 462°C (864°F).

## Exploration

Because Venus shines so brightly in the sky, people have studied it for thousands of years. The Mayans of ancient Mexico carefully **recorded** the planet's path in the sky.

Many spacecraft have explored Venus since the 1960s. Several spacecraft named *Venera* landed on Venus at different times and sent back pictures and **data** before being crushed by the atmosphere. Starting in 1990, the *Magellan* spacecraft orbited Venus and mapped the planet's surface with **technology** that could make images of what lies beneath Venus's clouds.

# Earth

Astronauts took this picture of
the Grand Canyon from space.

Earth is one of the rocky **planets**. It is the only **Solar System object** that we know has living things on it.

## Conditions

Earth has many different **surface features**, including mountains, flat plains, deep canyons, and ice caps. An ocean of water covers most of the surface. Earth's surface is always changing shape. Large sheets of rock, called plates, form the surface of Earth. These plates move slowly. As they move, the plates change Earth's surface features and create new ones. Moving wind and water also change Earth's surface features.

Earth has an **atmosphere** that is mostly **composed of** nitrogen gas. It also contains oxygen gas, which people need to survive. The atmosphere acts like a blanket holding heat around Earth. Without its atmosphere, Earth would be much colder. The coldest parts of Earth's surface can have **temperatures** as low as -88°C (-126°F). On the hottest parts of Earth, temperatures can be hotter than 58°C (136°F).

## Exploration

People have explored more of Earth than any other Solar System object, but not all of Earth has been explored. There are still many things we do not know about deep parts of the ocean. Satellites and spacecraft give us views of Earth that help us understand how the planet changes.

# Moon (Luna)

Astronauts landed this spacecraft on the surface of the Moon.

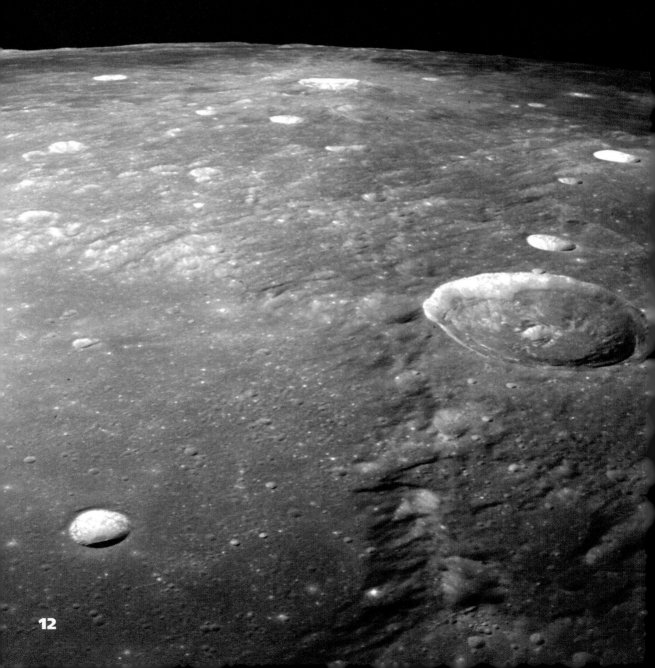

Earth's Moon is the only **Solar System object** that people have visited, other than Earth. It is named Luna (LOON-ah), but most people just call it the Moon. The Moon does not make its own light. Moonlight is light from the Sun that reflects off the Moon.

## Conditions

Even without a **telescope**, you can see light and dark places on the Moon. The dark places are flat plains that formed when lava hardened. The light places have many mountains and **craters**—holes left when objects hit the Moon's surface. These objects that have hit the Moon have broken much of its rocky surface into sand and dust.

The Moon has no **atmosphere** to hold in heat, and the **temperature** on the Moon's surface changes a great deal from day to night. When sunlight hits the Moon's surface, the temperature may be as hot as 123°C (253°F). However, it may be as cold as -233°C (-387°F) at night.

## Exploration

The Moon is the only object in space (other than Earth) that has been explored by humans. The Apollo **missions** sent a total of 12 astronauts to the Moon in the 1960s and 1970s. The Moon has also been explored by many other missions, including landers and **orbiting** spacecraft.

In 2009, a mission called LCROSS made a crash landing—on purpose! The spacecraft crashed into a deep crater on the Moon. The impact of the crash caused an explosion. By **observing** the explosion, scientists were able to tell that there is frozen water in the **lunar** soil at the bottom of the crater.

# Mars

The wheels of a rover made these tracks on the dusty surface of Mars. The rovers are robots that were sent to explore the red planet.

Mars is often called the red **planet**. From Earth, it looks like a bright, reddish **star**. Mars is one of the rocky planets.

## Conditions

Mars is covered with rocks. The surface of Mars is dry today, but scientists have found lots of **evidence** that liquid water once flowed there. The evidence includes **surface features** that look like dry riverbeds. The largest known mountain in the **Solar System** is a giant volcano on Mars. Mars also has canyons that are much longer and deeper than the Grand Canyon on Earth! Ice caps can be found at the two poles of Mars, just as on Earth. There are also many **craters** on the surface of Mars.

The **atmosphere** of Mars is mostly **composed of** carbon dioxide gas. It is much thinner than Earth's atmosphere. Mars's atmosphere has a very small amount of water, but it is enough to form some clouds, frost, and fog. The wind is very strong and can whip up lots of red dust. The dust can float in the air for months. This makes the sky look pink. The atmosphere of Mars does not block heat from the Sun during the day or keep warmth in at night the way Earth's atmosphere does. Mars is sometimes as cold as -87°C (-125°F), but the warmest place on Mars can reach a **temperature** of 20°C (68°F).

## Exploration

Many **missions** have explored Mars and studied rocks there. *Viking 1* and *2* both landed on Mars in 1976. The *Pathfinder* landed in 1997. The Mars **rovers** *Spirit* and *Opportunity* were sent to Mars in 2003. In 2008, the *Phoenix* spacecraft landed on Mars and gathered evidence about water there.

# Phobos

Phobos's largest crater
is about nine kilometers
(almost six miles) across

Phobos (FOE-bohs), one of the two known **moons** of Mars, is not **spherical** like many **Solar System objects**. It is small and shaped more like a potato.

## Conditions

Phobos has many **craters** on its rocky surface. Craters are holes made when objects hit the surface. The largest crater on Phobos is almost half as wide as Phobos itself!

When all those objects hit Phobos, they smashed much of its rocky surface into dust. The surface of Phobos is covered with a layer of dust about one meter (40 inches) thick! Landslides have left dark marks on the steep slopes of its huge craters.

Scientists think that a long time ago Phobos may have been an **asteroid**, until it was captured by Mars's **gravity** and became one of the moons of Mars.

Phobos has no **atmosphere** to hold heat on its surface, and **temperatures** on this little moon can drop as low as -112°C (-170°F).

## Exploration

Many spacecraft sent to explore Mars have also taken pictures of Phobos from space. *Viking 1* took close-up pictures of Phobos in 1978, and *Mars Global Surveyor* took photos in 1998 and 2003.

The Mars **rovers** *Spirit* and *Opportunity* have taken pictures of Phobos from the surface of Mars.

# Jupiter

**Great Red Spot
(a huge storm
on Jupiter)**

**a smaller
storm**

The reddish oval is a huge storm in Jupiter's
atmosphere. The lighter spots are smaller storms.

Jupiter (JOO-pit-ur) is the largest **planet** in the **Solar System**. It is bigger than all of the other planets put together! Jupiter is in the group of planets called **gas giants**, large planets that are mainly **composed of** gases.

## Conditions

Jupiter has a deep, thick **atmosphere**, which is mostly composed of hydrogen and helium gas. This layer of gas is very cloudy, and powerful storms are always happening there. Scientists have **observed** bolts of lightning in Jupiter's cloud tops. A giant storm called the Great Red Spot has been going on there for more than 340 years!

Underneath Jupiter's atmosphere is a huge ocean, but it is not an ocean of water like the ocean on Earth. Jupiter's ocean is composed of liquid hydrogen. The very center of Jupiter may contain a rocky core that is larger than Earth.

The center of Jupiter is very hot: about 24,000°C (43,000°F)! However, the high clouds can be as cold as -145°C (-229°F).

## Exploration

No spacecraft has ever landed on Jupiter. Jupiter's thick atmosphere would crush a spacecraft before it could land.

The *Voyager 1* and *2* spacecraft flew close to Jupiter and took pictures in 1979. The pictures showed that Jupiter has rings made of dust that can't be seen from Earth.

Starting in 1995, the *Galileo* spacecraft **orbited** Jupiter 34 times, taking pictures of the planet and its **moons**. *Galileo* released a smaller spacecraft that dropped into Jupiter's atmosphere. The spacecraft sent back **data** about **conditions** there. After a few hours, the spacecraft was crushed.

# Io

erupting
lava

This picture shows lava erupting
from the surface of Io.

Io (EYE-oh) is one of the **moons** that **orbit** Jupiter. Io has more active volcanoes than any other **Solar System object**.

## Conditions

The colorful, rocky surface of Io has many volcanoes. Hot, melted rock from inside Io shoots out in huge explosions that can reach more than 300 kilometers (190 miles) above the surface. Smooth, hardened lava covers most of Io's surface between the volcanoes. Io also has mountains that are higher than any mountains on Earth.

**Gravity** from Jupiter and its other moons causes Io's surface to bulge, squeeze, and stretch. This squeezing causes the heat within Io.

Near an erupting volcano, the **temperature** at the surface of Io may rise to 555°C (1,031°F) or hotter. Most of the moon's surface is very cold, however—as cold as -188°C (-306°F)! That is because Io has no **atmosphere** to hold heat near its surface.

## Exploration

The **astronomer** Galileo Galilei discovered Io and three other moons in 1610. The first close-up pictures of Io were taken by the *Voyager 1* and *2* spacecraft in 1979. In these pictures, scientists counted 200 volcanoes, nine of which were erupting at the same time! This was the first time scientists had **observed** volcanoes erupting anywhere in the **Solar System** other than on Earth.

# Europa

Scientists want to figure out how these cracks formed on the surface of Europa.

Europa (yur-OH-pah) is one of the **moons** that **orbit** Jupiter. Some people think Europa looks like a cracked eggshell because it has lines all over its surface.

## Conditions

There is a thick crust of ice on Europa. The surface is very smooth, but it is covered with lines that may be cracks in the ice. The smooth surface is **evidence** that new ice has formed in the last few million years. **Astronomers** have found evidence of giant ice plates that float and move around the surface of Europa.

Europa has no **atmosphere** to hold heat near its surface, so the **temperature** is about -160°C (-256°F) at the surface of this icy moon. However, the inside of Europa is probably much warmer.

Scientists have made **models** of Europa to figure out how its **surface features** may have formed. These models show that the cracks on Europa may be caused by melted or slushy water beneath the frozen surface. Europa has a hidden ocean of liquid water that could be more than 100 kilometers (about 60 miles) deep! However, scientists do not have enough evidence to know for sure how thick the icy crust is.

## Exploration

Europa is one of four moons discovered by the astronomer Galileo Galilei in 1610. Almost 400 years later, in 1995, the *Galileo* spacecraft flew past Europa and took pictures of its smooth, icy surface.

# Ganymede

Some parts of Ganymede are covered with craters. Other parts are smooth.

Ganymede (GAN-ih-meed) is the largest **moon** in the **Solar System**. It is larger than the **planet** Mercury! Ganymede **orbits** Jupiter.

## Conditions

Ganymede's surface is **composed of** icy material. If you look at pictures of Ganymede's surface, you can see dark parts and light parts. The dark parts have different **surface features** than the light parts. The dark parts are covered with **craters**, which are holes left by objects that hit the surface. The light parts have long ridges and grooves. There are only a few craters on the light parts.

On **Solar System objects**, older surfaces have more craters. The large number of craters on the dark parts of Ganymede is **evidence** that these parts are older than the light parts. The evidence shows that, millions of years ago, the surface of Ganymede broke apart and moved around. New material flowed up from under the surface and hardened. That new material formed the light parts of Ganymede's surface.

Ganymede does not have an **atmosphere**, and the **temperature** on the surface of Ganymede is very cold: about -120°C (-184°F).

## Exploration

Along with three other moons of Jupiter, Ganymede was discovered by the **astronomer** Galileo Galilei in 1610. Almost 400 years later, the *Galileo* spacecraft flew past Ganymede on its trip to Jupiter in 1995 and took pictures that show Ganymede's different surface features.

# Callisto

These craters formed when objects hit the surface of Callisto.

Callisto (cal-ISS-toe) is one of the many **moons** that **orbit** Jupiter. Callisto is a large moon, almost as big as the **planet** Mercury.

## Conditions

Callisto's surface is mostly ice and rock. The surface is covered with **craters**—holes made by objects that hit Callisto. Callisto has more craters than any other **Solar System object**.

There are no volcanoes or earthquakes on Callisto. Because of this, the surface of Callisto has not changed much in billions of years. This makes Callisto unlike other large Solar System objects, whose surfaces have changed a lot and are still changing.

Callisto has no **atmosphere** to help keep its surface warm. **Temperatures** on Callisto can be as cold as -190°C (-310°F).

## Exploration

In 1610, the **astronomer** Galileo Galilei discovered four moons, including Callisto.

No spacecraft have landed on Callisto, but many have flown past this moon. The *Galileo* spacecraft came the closest. It flew past Callisto eight times between 1994 and 2003, taking lots of close-up pictures of Callisto's surface.

# Saturn

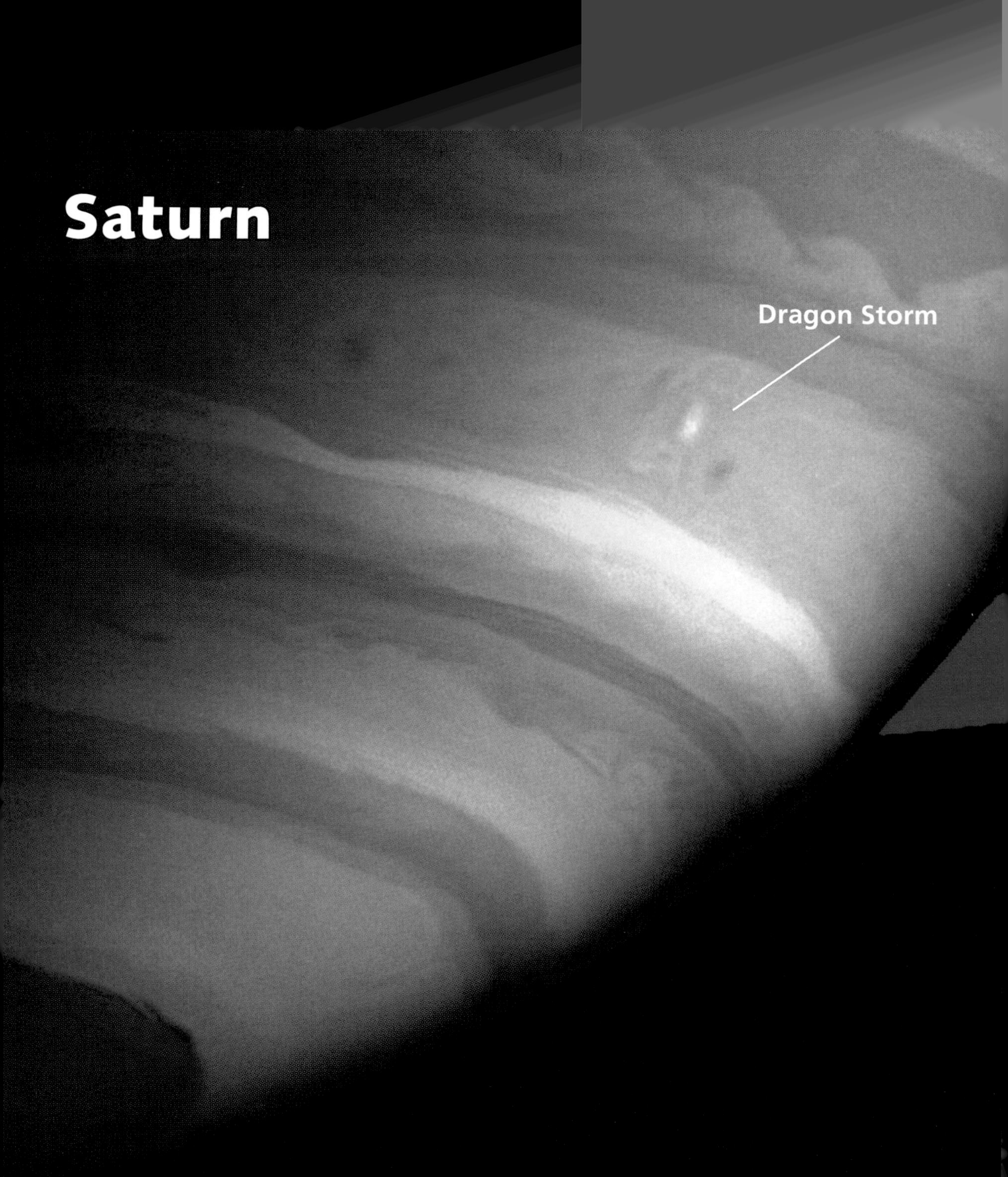

Dragon Storm

This picture shows a storm in Saturn's atmosphere. Scientists named it the Dragon Storm because of its shape.

Saturn (SAT-urn) is the second largest **planet** in the **Solar System**. Saturn is one of the **gas giants**, large planets that are mainly **composed of** gases. This huge planet has rings around it that are made of bits of icy rock. Some of these bits of rock are as small as a piece of dust, and some are as big as a house.

## Conditions

Saturn's deep, thick **atmosphere** is mostly composed of hydrogen and helium gas. Winds blow very fast in Saturn's atmosphere—about 1,600 kilometers per hour (990 miles per hour). Winds and rising heat create the yellow stripes that can be seen in the cloud tops. The thick clouds hide everything beneath them.

Deeper inside Saturn is an ocean of liquid hydrogen and helium. Saturn probably has a rocky core at its center.

The **temperature** at Saturn's center is about 15,000°C (27,000°F). However, the temperature at the cloud tops can be as cold as -175°C (-283°F).

## Exploration

Spacecraft cannot land on Saturn because they would be crushed by the thick atmosphere. *Voyager 1* and *2* flew past Saturn and took pictures in the early 1980s. In 1997, the *Cassini* spacecraft was sent toward Saturn. It took seven years to get there. *Cassini* began **orbiting** Saturn on June 30, 2004, and has been sending back pictures and **data** ever since.

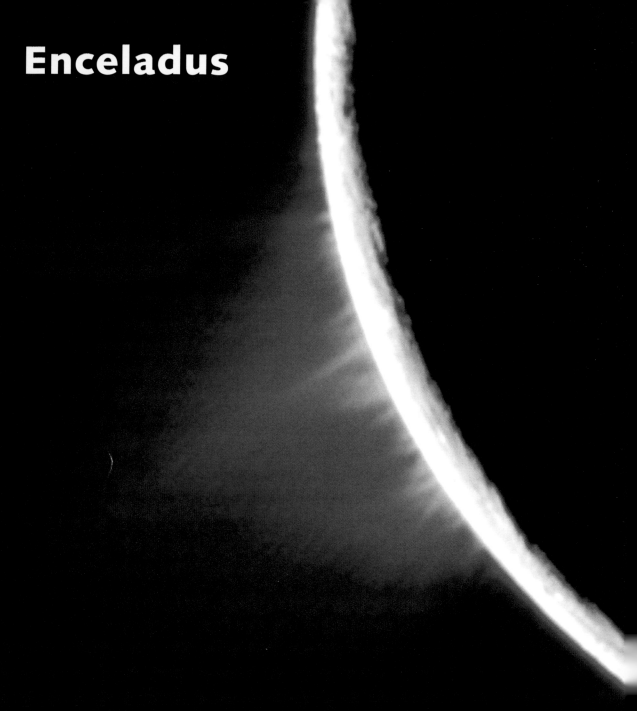

# Enceladus

This picture shows huge fountains of ice shooting out of the surface of Enceladus.

Enceladus (en-SELL-ah-dus) is one of the **moons** that **orbit** Saturn. The icy surface of Enceladus reflects almost all of the sunlight that hits it. That means Enceladus would look very bright if you flew near it in a spacecraft.

## Conditions

The surface of Enceladus is **composed of** ice. Some parts of Enceladus have very different **surface features** than other parts. In some places, Enceladus has many **craters**—holes made when objects hit the surface. Other parts of Enceladus are smooth, with no craters at all. These smooth parts are **evidence** that new ice has formed on the surface.

Huge fountains of ice shoot up from Enceladus, like lava shooting from a volcano. This may be evidence of liquid water beneath the frozen surface. These ice fountains come from four huge cracks on the surface that look like stripes.

Gases come out of the ice fountains and form a thin layer of gas around Enceladus. The layer of gas is thinner in some places than in others. There is not very much gas, so the layer is not really an **atmosphere**.

Enceladus is very cold. The **temperature** at the surface is about -200°C (-328°F).

## Exploration

The spacecraft *Cassini* has flown by Enceladus many times since 2005 and taken close-up pictures of Enceladus's surface features. *Cassini* also collected evidence that shows where some of the ice shooting out of Enceladus is going: one of Saturn's rings! The ring is made of tiny pieces of ice that come from Enceladus.

# Titan

Titan's lakes have no water in them. They are composed of liquid methane.

Titan (TIE-tan) is the largest **moon** of Saturn. Clouds hide the surface of Titan. Besides Earth, Titan is the only **Solar System object** we know of that has lakes on its surface.

## Conditions

Titan's surface is mostly solid ice, but parts of the surface are covered by large lakes. The lakes are **composed of** liquid methane, not water. Other **surface features** on Titan are sand dunes, cliffs, and canyons.

Clouds hide the surface of Titan. Other moons in the **Solar System** have little or no **atmosphere**, but Titan has an atmosphere that is thicker than Earth's! Like Earth's atmosphere, Titan's atmosphere is mostly composed of nitrogen gas. However, the atmosphere of Titan has no oxygen, so people could not breathe there. Because Titan is so far from the Sun, this moon is very cold. The **temperature** on the surface is about -179°C (-290°F).

## Exploration

The spacecraft *Voyager 1* flew past Titan in 1980 and took pictures with a camera, but only thick clouds could be seen.

In 2004, a spacecraft named *Cassini* began **orbiting** Saturn. *Cassini* used different **technology** to make images of Titan's surface through the clouds. These images were the first to show liquid lakes.

*Cassini* carried a probe spacecraft called *Huygens*. In 2005, the *Huygens* probe separated from the *Cassini* spacecraft and entered the thick atmosphere of Titan. It was able to land safely on the surface and kept working for more than an hour. *Huygens* took pictures and **recorded** weather **conditions**.

**33**

# Uranus

**This is a view of the night side of Uranus.**

Uranus (YUR-an-us or yoo-RAY-nus) is one of the **gas giants**, large **planets** that are mainly **composed of** gases. One strange thing about Uranus is the way it **rotates**. Other planets spin from side to side, but Uranus rolls from top to bottom. Uranus's **axis** may have become tilted when another large object hit the planet.

## Conditions

Uranus has a deep, thick **atmosphere** that is composed of hydrogen and helium gas. Beneath the atmosphere may be a deep, partly frozen ocean composed of water, ammonia, and methane. Uranus probably has a rocky core at its center.

The top of Uranus's atmosphere is very cold—about -215°C (-355°F). However, **temperatures** at the planet's center may be hotter than 7,000°C (12,600°F). There are at least 11 thin, black rings around Uranus. These rings are made of ice and fine dust. They are very thin and difficult to see.

## Exploration

In 1986, the spacecraft *Voyager 2* took pictures of Uranus. Nothing was visible beneath the thick atmosphere. *Voyager 2* also took the first close-up pictures of the planet's rings and **moons**.

# Miranda

Some canyons on Miranda's surface are V-shaped.

Miranda (mih-RAN-dah) is a **moon** that **orbits** Uranus. This small moon looks very strange. Its **surface features** seem to be all mixed up.

## Conditions

Miranda's surface is **composed of** ice and rock. Miranda has surface features that look like huge rocky steps. It has canyons that are as deep as 20 kilometers (about 12 miles). Some of the canyons are big V shapes. Miranda also has **craters**—holes left when objects hit the surface. All of these features on Miranda's surface are jumbled together.

Scientists have different ideas about why Miranda looks the way it does. Miranda may have broken apart and come back together again. Or it may be that the inside of Miranda became hot and parts of it melted. Scientists need more **evidence** to understand Miranda's surface better.

Miranda is a very cold moon with no **atmosphere**. The **temperature** on the surface of Miranda is about -180°C (-292°F).

## Exploration

A spacecraft called *Voyager 2* took close-up pictures of Miranda in 1986 as the spacecraft flew past on its way to Neptune. Exploring Miranda was not the main goal of this **mission**, but scientists were able to learn about this moon's strange surface from the pictures.

# Neptune

These are white clouds at the top of Neptune's thick, blue atmosphere.

Neptune (NEP-toon) is one of the **gas giants**, large **planets** that are mainly **composed of** gases. Around Neptune are five thin, dark rings that are made of bits of rock, ice, and dust. The rings may be pieces left over from **comets** or **asteroids** that hit Neptune's **moons**.

## Conditions

Neptune has a deep, thick **atmosphere** that is mostly composed of hydrogen and helium gas. Neptune's atmosphere is very cloudy. The thick clouds hide everything beneath them.

Winds on Neptune can blow as fast as 2,000 kilometers per hour (about 1,200 miles per hour)—faster than on any other planet. Huge storms have been **observed** in Neptune's atmosphere. One storm was so big that Earth could fit inside it!

Beneath its atmosphere, Neptune probably has an ocean of liquid water, ammonia, and methane. The planet probably also has a rocky core. The center of Neptune is hot—up to 5,150°C (9,300°F). The top of Neptune's atmosphere is very cold, however. At the cloud tops, the **temperature** is -218°C (-360°F).

## Exploration

Scientists discovered Neptune by **investigating** the planet Uranus. How? By investigating the **orbit** of Uranus, scientists found that **gravity** from another planet was pulling on Uranus. Using math, they were able to figure out where that planet would be. **Astronomers** used **telescopes** to observe that part of space, and in 1846, they found Neptune. The spacecraft *Voyager 2* flew past Neptune in 1989 and took pictures of the planet. The pictures also showed six moons no one had known about before.

# Triton

**Some parts of Triton's surface look like the skin of a cantaloupe melon.**

Triton (TRY-tun) is the largest **moon** that **orbits** Neptune. This moon is the coldest **Solar System object** we know of.

## Conditions

Long ridges and valleys cross Triton's icy surface. Fountains of gas and dust sometimes shoot out of the moon's surface. These fountains can reach up to eight kilometers (almost five miles) high!

Triton has an **atmosphere** that is mostly **composed of** nitrogen gas, like Earth's. However, Triton's atmosphere is much, much thinner than Earth's atmosphere. Triton has the coldest surface **temperature** that has ever been **recorded** in the **Solar System**: -235°C (-391°F).

Neptune's moons all orbit the **planet** in the same direction—except Triton. Triton orbits in the opposite direction. Triton may once have been an object that orbited the Sun on its own, but it was captured long ago by Neptune's **gravity**.

## Exploration

In 1989, *Voyager 2* flew past Triton and sent lots of **data** back to Earth about Triton's size, color, clouds, temperature, and **composition**, and how fast it **rotates**.

# What Else Is in Our Solar System?

There are thousands of other objects in our **Solar System**, including the Sun, **asteroids**, **comets**, and Kuiper Belt objects (KBOs), as well as lots of dust.

## The Sun

The Sun is the only **star** in our Solar System. It is a huge **sphere** of gas that gives off heat and light. The Sun is at the center of our Solar System, and the **planets** and many other objects **orbit**, or **revolve** around, the Sun.

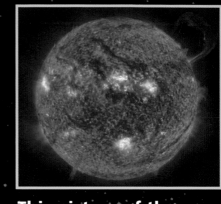

This picture of the Sun was taken with a special **telescope** that shows features on the surface of the Sun.

## Asteroids

Like planets, asteroids orbit the Sun, but asteroids are much smaller than planets. The largest asteroid is almost 1,000 kilometers (about 620 miles) across, and the smallest ones are smaller than a school bus. Many asteroids have strange shapes: they are often long and lumpy. Scientists have discovered hundreds of thousands of asteroids in our Solar System. Most asteroids orbit in the Asteroid Belt, an area between the orbits of Mars and Jupiter.

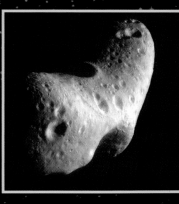

These asteroids have different shapes and sizes.

# Comets

Comets are like dirty snowballs that orbit the Sun. As they orbit the Sun, comets are sometimes closer to the Sun and sometimes farther away. A comet is coldest when it is farthest from the Sun. When a comet gets close to the Sun, sunlight warms up the comet. The warmed-up comet gives off lots of gas and dust, which can be seen from Earth as a glowing tail.

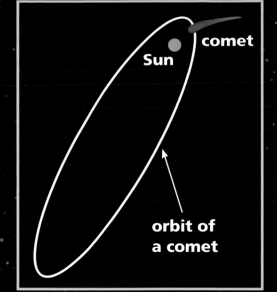

**orbit of a comet**

**a comet as seen from Earth**

# KBOs

Kuiper (KY-per) Belt objects, or KBOs, are **Solar System objects** that orbit the Sun in the Kuiper Belt, an area beyond the outermost planet, Neptune. KBOs are mostly **composed of** ice. No spacecraft has passed close enough to a KBO to take a clear picture yet, but a spacecraft will arrive at the Kuiper Belt in 2015.

**An artist imagined what one of the largest KBOs might look like.**

# Planet and Moon Data Tables

| Solar System object | What is it? | Diameter | Surface gravity compared to Earth's |
|---|---|---|---|
| Mercury | planet | about 4,880 kilometers | only $\frac{1}{3}$ as strong as Earth's gravity |
| Venus | planet | about 12,100 kilometers | slightly weaker than Earth's gravity |
| Earth | planet | about 12,760 kilometers | |
| Moon (Luna) | moon | about 3,470 kilometers | only $\frac{1}{6}$ as strong as Earth's gravity |
| Mars | planet | about 6,790 kilometers | only $\frac{1}{3}$ as strong as Earth's gravity |
| Phobos | moon | 27 kilometers across (Phobos is not a sphere.) | less than $\frac{1}{1,000}$ as strong as Earth's gravity |
| Jupiter | planet | about 142,980 kilometers | more than twice as strong as Earth's gravity |
| Io | moon | about 3,640 kilometers | only $\frac{1}{6}$ as strong as Earth's gravity |
| Europa | moon | about 3,130 kilometers | only $\frac{1}{7}$ as strong as Earth's gravity |
| Ganymede | moon | about 5,270 kilometers | only $\frac{1}{7}$ as strong as Earth's gravity |
| Callisto | moon | about 4,810 kilometers | only $\frac{1}{8}$ as strong as Earth's gravity |
| Saturn | planet | about 120,540 kilometers | slightly weaker than Earth's gravity |
| Enceladus | moon | about 490 kilometers | only $\frac{1}{87}$ as strong as Earth's gravity |
| Titan | moon | about 5,150 kilometers | only $\frac{1}{7}$ as strong as Earth's gravity |
| Uranus | planet | about 51,120 kilometers | slightly weaker than Earth's gravity |
| Miranda | moon | about 480 kilometers | only $\frac{1}{124}$ as strong as Earth's gravity |
| Neptune | planet | about 49,530 kilometers | slightly stronger than Earth's gravity |
| Triton | moon | about 2,700 kilometers | only $\frac{1}{13}$ as strong as Earth's gravity |

| Planet | Distance from the Sun | Time it takes to orbit the Sun | Time it takes to rotate once | Number of moons |
|---|---|---|---|---|
| Mercury | about 58 million kilometers | about 88 Earth days | about 59 Earth days | none |
| Venus | about 108 million kilometers | about 225 Earth days | about 243 Earth days | none |
| Earth | about 150 million kilometers | 365 Earth days | one Earth day | one moon |
| Mars | about 228 million kilometers | about 687 Earth days | about 25 hours | two small moons |
| Jupiter | about 778 million kilometers | about 12 Earth years | about 10 hours | four large moons and at least 59 smaller ones |
| Saturn | about 1 billion 427 million kilometers | about 29 Earth years | about 11 hours | at least 60 moons, some large, some small |
| Uranus | about 2 billion 871 million kilometers | about 84 Earth years | about 17 hours | at least 27 moons |
| Neptune | about 4 billion 498 million kilometers | about 165 Earth years | about 16 hours | one large moon and at least 12 smaller ones |

| Moon | Planet it orbits | Distance from the planet | Time it takes to orbit the planet | Time it takes to rotate once |
|---|---|---|---|---|
| Moon (Luna) | Earth | about 384,400 kilometers | about 27 Earth days | about 27 Earth days |
| Phobos | Mars | about 9,400 kilometers | just over seven hours | just under 25 hours |
| Io | Jupiter | about 422,000 kilometers | about two Earth days | about two Earth days |
| Europa | Jupiter | about 671,000 kilometers | about four Earth days | about four Earth days |
| Ganymede | Jupiter | about 1,070,000 kilometers | about seven Earth days | about seven Earth days |
| Callisto | Jupiter | about 1,883,000 kilometers | about 17 Earth days | about 17 Earth days |
| Enceladus | Saturn | about 238,000 kilometers | a little more than one Earth day | a little more than one Earth day |
| Titan | Saturn | about 1,222,000 kilometers | about 16 Earth days | about 16 Earth days |
| Miranda | Uranus | about 129,900 kilometers | about one and a half Earth days | about one and a half Earth days |
| Triton | Neptune | about 354,800 kilometers | about six Earth days | about six Earth days |

# Glossary

**asteroid:** a piece of rock that orbits the Sun and is smaller than a planet

**astronomer:** a scientist who studies objects in space

**atmosphere:** the air or gas around a planet or moon

**axis:** the center line around which something rotates

**comet:** a Solar System object that is made of dust, rock, and ice, and that sometimes has a tail of dust and gases

**composed of:** made of

**composition:** what something is made of

**conditions:** what it is like in a certain place, such as the temperature, strength of gravity, and weather in that place

**crater:** a hole made by an object that hit the surface of a planet, moon, or other Solar System object

**data:** information collected in an investigation

**diameter:** the distance across a circle or sphere measured from one side, through the center, to the opposite side.

**evidence:** clues that help explain something or answer a question

**exploration:** the attempt to discover new things about a place

**gas giant:** a large planet composed mainly of gases

**gravity:** the force that pulls things down

**investigate:** to study or try to learn more about something

**lunar:** having to do with the Moon

**mission:** a project sending people or machines to gather new information about a place

**model:** an object, a diagram, or a computer program that helps us understand something by making it simpler or easier to see

**moon:** a large natural object that orbits a planet or any Solar System object other than the Sun

**observe:** to use any of the five senses to gather information about something

**orbit** (verb): to move around an object in space
(noun): the path an object takes when it moves around another object in space

**planet:** a large, ball-shaped object that orbits a star

**record:** to write down information

**revolve:** to orbit

**rotate:** to spin

**rover:** a robot designed to move around the surface of a Solar System object

**Solar System:** the Sun and the group of objects that orbit it

**Solar System object:** a moon, the Sun, or something that orbits the Sun, such as a planet, asteroid, or comet

**sphere:** anything that is shaped like a ball

**spherical:** shaped like a ball

**star:** a huge ball of gas that gives off heat and light

**surface feature:** something on the outside of a planet or moon, such as a crater, an ocean, or a volcano

**technology:** tools or machines designed for a specific purpose using scientific knowledge

**telescope:** a tool for observing objects that are very far away

**temperature:** how hot or cold something is

# Index

The page numbers in **bold** are the main entry for that planet or moon.